Escape from

Pyramid X

Dan Jolley

illustrated by Matt Wendt

LERNER · · · · POLIS

Story by Dan Jolley

Pencils and inks by Matt Wendt

Colouring by Hi-Fi Design

Lettering by Marshall Dillon and Terri Delgado

Graphic Universe™ is a trademark and Twisted Journeys® is a registered trademark
of Lerner Publishing Group, Inc.

First published in the United Kingdom in 2009 by
Lerner Books,
Dalton House,
60 Windsor Avenue,
London SW19 2RR

Website address: www.lernerbooks.co.uk

This edition was updated and edited for UK publication by Discovery Books Ltd.,
Unit 3, 37 Watling Street, Leintwardine, Shropshire SY7 0LW

British Library Cataloguing in Publication Data

Escape from Pyramid X. - (Twisted journeys)
1. Mummies - Comic books, strips, etc. - Juvenile fiction
2. Pyramids - Comic books, strips, etc. - Juvenile fiction
3. Adventure stories 4. Children's stories - Comic books,
strips, etc.
741.5

ISBN-13: 978 1 58013 493 4

Printed in China

ARE YOU READY FOR YOUR *Twisted Journeys®?*

YOU ARE THE HERO OF THE BOOK YOU'RE ABOUT TO READ. IT'S PACKED WITH ADVENTURES IN AN ANCIENT EGYPTIAN PYRAMID. AND EVERY STORY STARS *YOU!*

EACH PAGE TELLS WHAT HAPPENS TO *YOU* AS YOU EXPLORE THE PYRAMID, FACING DANGERS YOU NEVER EXPECTED. *YOUR* WORDS AND THOUGHTS ARE SHOWN IN THE *YELLOW BALLOONS*. AND YOU GET TO DECIDE WHAT HAPPENS NEXT. JUST FOLLOW THE NOTE AT THE BOTTOM OF EACH PAGE UNTIL YOU REACH A *Twisted Journeys®* PAGE. THEN MAKE THE CHOICE *YOU* LIKE BEST.

BUT BE CAREFUL...THE WRONG CHOICE COULD MAKE YOUR EXPLORING DAYS VERY SHORT!

Egypt!

You still can't believe you won first prize in the essay contest. Here you are with the sand under your feet and the dry desert wind in your hair. It seems like a dream to be going on a dig this huge. And with someone as famous as the brilliant archaeologist Professor Emil Snackport! You're one of only six students from around the world selected for this honour.

'Come along, right this way,' the guide says. 'No pushing. Single-file line.'

You peep around two big children chatting in German. There it is! Huge and dark against the starry night sky — Pyramid X! It was only recently uncovered and it's supposed to be unlike any of the other great pyramids in Egypt. It hasn't even been fully explored yet. Who knows what kinds of secrets and mysteries it might hold?

GO ON TO THE NEXT PAGE.

Professor Snackport heads for Pyramid X. You and the other children follow him . . .

. . . and soon you see a dark, creepy doorway right at ground level.

'You're some of the luckiest children on Earth!' Professor Snackport says. 'There are so many rumours about this pyramid! Some say it's the home of ruthless, evil creatures. Or that strange wizards built it with ancient magic. Some even say that the hieroglyphs inside are magical themselves!'

He looks around at the group, eager and excited.

'I suppose we'll find out soon, won't we, children?'

Professor Snackport ducks inside.

You and the other students have no choice but to follow the professor . . .

. . . into a long, stone hallway. Everyone else is ahead of you. But off to your left, you see a small, dark, mysterious passageway. What could be down there . . . ?

6

GO ON TO THE NEXT PAGE.

You are here to learn . . .
but you also want some adventure!

WILL YOU . . .

. . . follow the professor and the
other students?
TURN TO PAGE 54.

. . . leave the group and duck
down the side passageway?
TURN TO PAGE 18.

Once you get a good hold on the fabric it rips easily enough. The sack falls away. You're free . . .

. . . and completely lost!

You're in a room you don't recognize . . . but there's only one door. You creep through it and down another stone corridor.

Soon you see another doorway next to a stack of wooden planks. There's a big, heavy stone door here, open just a few centimetres. You get closer still . . . and you hear the thieves' voices again. You inch forwards and peep around the corner.

The five men are standing near a treasure chest made of gold, with more gold and jewels inside it. They're arguing. . .

Then you spot something that you're pretty sure they haven't noticed. There's a square stone sticking out of the wall just a tiny bit. You think it's some kind of switch.

And the ceiling in that room looks like it's just waiting to drop down. . .

GO ON TO THE NEXT PAGE.

You've seen enough movies to know places like this are often filled with traps.

WILL YOU . . .

. . . decide to play it safe and just wedge the stone door closed?
TURN TO PAGE 88.

. . . take a chance and hit the switch in the wall?
TURN TO PAGE 111.

'We can't risk going in there,' you hear yourself say.
'I think we should stay here and deal with the mummy ourselves.'

The other kids are scared, but they agree with you.

'Yeah,' Kajal says. 'It's seven against one, right? We can take him!'

Professor Snackport doesn't look convinced. But before he can say anything, you hear the mummy approaching.

Shuffle-scrape. Shuffle-scrape. Shuffle-scrape.

The mummy comes around a corner. His eyes light up with an evil glow.

'Pitiful little children,' he grunts. His voice sounds like bits of gravel crunching together. 'You come into my pyramid — my home — and think you can *escape me?*'

KLICK

OH NO-- **OH NO**! EVERYONE MOVE! WE'VE GOT TO GET OUT OF HERE BEFORE--

BOOOM

NOW YOU'LL SEE WHAT IT FEELS LIKE TO BE LOCKED IN A TOMB FOREVER!

HAHAHAHAHAHAAAA!

THE END

11

In less than a second you've slipped the amulet away from the thief . . .

. . . but then you've got more to worry about: The stairway leads into a dank, dimly lit square chamber, like part of a dungeon. The only thing in it is a statue that looks like an Egyptian queen.

'Okay, kid,' one of the thieves says. 'Go over there. Take a look.'

You approach the statue cautiously . . . and suddenly the amulet begins to glow. The same glow is shining out of the statue's eyes.

Before you even realise what's happening, you're transformed! Your skin is dry and brittle, but you feel strong — and your clothes have changed to ancient Egyptian armour.

'Look!' one of the thieves exclaims. 'The kid's turned into some kind of mummy warrior!'

He's right! There's a spear in your hand — and you want to do whatever the statue tells you to.

You can hear the statue's voice in your head, telling you to put on the amulet. And she's got three tasks for you! Which will you choose first?

WILL YOU . . .

. . . start looking for people to transform into other mummy warriors?
TURN TO PAGE 39.

. . . scare everyone out of the pyramid — thieves, students and all?
TURN TO PAGE 50.

. . . force the thieves to return what they've stolen?
TURN TO PAGE 78.

GO ON TO THE NEXT PAGE.

'This isn't happening,' says Lars. 'It can't be happening! Mummies aren't *real!* All of this is just some kind of strange dream!'

But the mummy soldiers in the doorway definitely *look* real. They pause and glare at you. Then they step aside to make room for their master. The mummy wearing the amulet steps through his ranks into the room.

'All those who knew me when I was alive knew my power. Now *you* shall know it as well.'

The torchlight glints off gleaming blades. The mummy steps back out of the room . . . and as the door closes, sealing you in for eternity, the soldiers step forwards . . .

. . . and raise their swords.

THE END

Why would you believe anything a thief tells you?

'HELLLPP MEEEEEEE! SOMEBODY HELLLPP MEEEEEEE!'

Instants later you hear a familiar voice. 'Good heavens!' Professor Snackport says, untying the sack. 'However did you get in there?'

You jump up and look around, blinking. You're in a small, unfamiliar room. Professor Snackport stands a short distance away. He looks worried.

'Professor! You won't believe what happened! I saw these men and they were *stealing stuff* and we've got to go tell the police!'

The professor's worried look doesn't change. He says, 'Good heavens,' again. You're starting to wonder why he's not more upset.

That's when the thief who grabbed you walks in and stands next to the professor. 'Well, Emil?' the thief says. 'What should we do with your student?'

'Well, we've got no choice,' the professor says. He looks straight at you. 'You'll have to join us, won't you?'

GO ON TO THE NEXT PAGE.

You're stunned! You can't believe the famous Professor Snackport is working with dangerous criminals — criminals who might do you serious harm!

WILL YOU . . .

. . . play along and agree
to join up with them?
TURN TO PAGE 35.

. . . make a break and run for it?
TURN TO PAGE 90.

You didn't come all the way to Egypt just to listen to a boring lecture! So you drop back and wait in a dark corner. When the group has gone far enough . . .

. . . you dart across the corridor and enter the side passage. Professor Snackport said parts of this pyramid hadn't been explored yet, right? Maybe you'll find something nobody's ever found before.

The passage is very narrow and lit by torches. A few times your shoulders brush the walls on both sides. It takes a couple of sharp turns . . .

. . . and then you hear voices ahead! They sound like they're just around the next corner. You peer around the bend and see a curtain hanging across the passageway. There's a flicker of candlelight beyond it. It sounds like several men are talking quietly.

You creep forwards.

GO ON TO THE NEXT PAGE.

GO ON TO THE NEXT PAGE.

These guys clearly don't belong here.

WILL YOU . . .

. . . go back to tell someone in authority about them?

TURN TO PAGE 67.

. . . go through the curtain and confront them?

TURN TO PAGE 42.

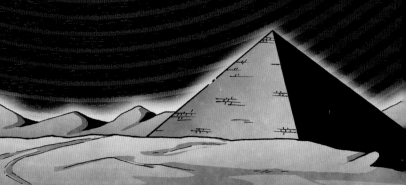

'It's okay!' you shout. 'It's okay! It's me!'

Seconds later the group is clustered around you, helping you peel the rest of the bandages away. 'I say!' Professor Snackport exclaims. 'How did this happen? Where have you been?'

Within an hour you're standing outside Pyramid X, watching the thieves being taken away by the Egyptian police. The local police chief finishes talking to Professor Snackport and then comes over to you. 'Fine job you did in there,' he tells you as he shakes your hand. 'Those men would have robbed this site of some truly priceless treasures. I only have one question."

'Yes, sir?'

'What about those *bandages?* I don't understand where they came from.'

You shrug. 'Honestly, sir, I don't either. If someone else wants to find out, it's fine with me. But I am *not* going back in that pyramid.'

And that's final.

THE END

You and the thieves come out of the stairwell into a room about the size of your living room at home. There's another doorway on the opposite wall. This place looks more like a dungeon than anything else. It's dark, smelly, a little damp and only lit by one torch on the wall. Except dungeons don't usually have beautiful, perfectly carved statues of ancient Egyptian queens sticking up out of the floor. And this one does.

'Who's that?' you ask.

A thief prods you in the back with something sharp. 'Quiet,' he barks. 'You know as much about this as we do.'

The biggest thief grins at you. 'But that's about to change, because you're going to examine that piece for us.' He puts his hand between your shoulder blades and practically shoves you towards the statue.

GO ON TO THE NEXT PAGE.

You're not totally sure what's just happened to you —
but you know it's the weirdest thing you've ever felt.
In fact, you feel as if you're kind of . . . frightening.

WILL YOU . . .

. . . take a closer look at that statue?
TURN TO PAGE 86.

. . . run away so you can take
some time to think about this?
TURN TO PAGE 91.

...attack the thieves?
TURN TO PAGE 110.

You take a deep breath and face the approaching mummy.

'Grind up your bones,' the mummy hisses. Another few seconds and it'll be within reach. 'Grind them all up!'

'What do we do?' Professor Snackport wails from right behind you. He's trembling with fear. 'I don't want to die!'

'We do *this*!' you shout – and you kick down one of the big wooden ceiling supports.

For a moment nothing happens.

But then a grinding noise in the ceiling makes the mummy look up! A huge block of stone slides out of place . . .

. . . and *falls* – directly onto the mummy.

He's squashed flat.

'Is that it?' the professor asks. 'Is it over?'

You shrug . . .

. . . but it actually *is* over. You can tell it is.

Just like you can tell you're going to get a very good mark from Professor Snackport.

THE END

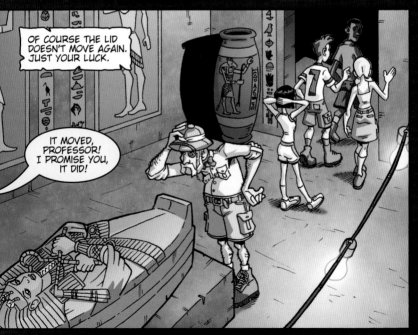

GO ON TO THE NEXT PAGE.

'Yes, well,' the professor says. He clears his throat. 'Why don't you help me open this lid and we'll see what we can see?'

Right now that is the absolutely, positively *last* thing you want to do. But you don't see any way around it. You help the professor push the big, heavy lid to one side.

'Well, now,' Professor Snackport says. 'Hmm. Hmmm.'

You don't want to look inside. You *really* don't. But you can't *help* yourself.

Taking a deep breath, you peek over the edge. . .

GO ON TO THE NEXT PAGE.

Inside the sarcophagus is a mummy. Ancient. Dried up. Covered in old ragged bandages. You think when he was alive the mummy must have been a big, powerful man. But now . . .

He's obviously been dead for a very long time. Maybe you did imagine the lid moving . . . ?

The mummy's still scary. You don't want to get any closer to it. . . But around its neck is a beautiful amulet made of gold and some gorgeous blue stone.

Professor Snackport doesn't seem to notice the amulet. He's paying more attention to the mummy's feet.

'Fascinating,' says the professor. 'Size nine and a half, I'd say. . .'

That amulet looks awfully important.

WILL YOU . . .

. . . keep quiet and stay away from the mummy?
TURN TO PAGE 94.

. . . draw the professor's attention to it?
TURN TO PAGE 71.

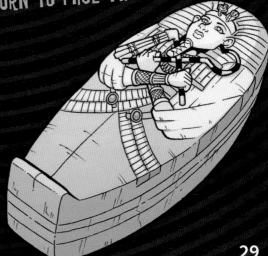

You take a huge gulp of air and then scream louder than you've ever screamed before.

'*Help! Help me! Help!*' Surely the professor will hear you – surely someone will!

But instead you see the mummy's head swivel towards you – and the glowing eyes narrow as it spots you there in the corner.

'So I have *you* to thank for releasing me!"

You can't help but stare as it climbs out of the sarcophagus. 'How thoughtful of you . . .' it says in its horrible voice,'. . . to remain here for me. You shall become my *first meal!*'

You try to scream again, but the mummy moves too quickly. Before you can react at all its hands close around your throat – and for you, this is clearly

THE END

As soon as you slide the amulet over your head you feel power flowing through you. *Amazing* power. This mummy was meant to be a guardian. A *protector*.

You turn and face the first mummy as it slides and scrapes into the room.

'You can't stop me!' it snarls. 'Not even with the ancient power!'

But you know the mummy couldn't be more wrong. You raise one hand. It suddenly shines with a bright golden light and a beam of *sunlight* surges out from your fingertips! The sunbeam strikes the mummy squarely in the chest —

— and the mummy *crumbles into dust!*

Suddenly everything is silent.

Everyone steps back away from you, staring.

The amulet falls from your neck and clunks on the stone floor. You know the danger is over — that Pyramid X is safe now.

Wow. 'Young Child Saves Fellow Students' Lives' will look *great* in the school newspaper!

THE END

Dear Mum and Dad,
A funny thing happened on the way to the dig today...

The square of stone with the cat's head symbol on it moves back into the pedestal. At first you think that's all that's happening . . .

. . . but then you feel the floor begin to tremble. You look around at the thieves. They're backing out of the room. You try to follow them, but one of them shouts: 'Stay where you are, kid! You're our guinea pig, remember?'

The whole room starts to descend, like a big lift. It takes a few minutes before you come to rest. Then you find yourself in a long, narrow room with a beautiful solid gold sarcophagus at one end. It's propped up, so you can see the lid. It looks like there's a carving of a gorgeous Egyptian queen on it.

Halfway between you and the sarcophagus there's a doorway in one wall. It could be a way out. . .

You want nothing more than to get out of here. But that coffin looks *so* cool . . . !

WILL YOU . . .

. . . approach the sarcophagus for a better look?
TURN TO PAGE 36.

. . . take the doorway and try to escape this craziness?
TURN TO PAGE 103.

OKAY, WHAT IS THIS? IT'S SOME KIND OF *TRICK*, ISN'T IT?

YOU KNOW IT'S A TRICK. IT'S GOT TO BE.

I CAN UNDERSTAND HOW YOU MIGHT THINK SO. MY APPEARANCE MUST BE QUITE *FRIGHTFUL*.

TRULY, IT'S ALL RIGHT.

ALLOW ME TO INTRODUCE MYSELF. MY NAME IS *PRINCE AMENHOTEP*.

BUT... BUT...

SO YOU FELL DOWN THIS CHUTE, DID YOU? HMM. DOWN FROM THE WORLD OUTSIDE.

I'M *VERY* INTERESTED IN WHAT THE WORLD HAS BECOME WHILE I SLEPT.

DO YOU THINK YOU COULD INTRODUCE ME TO IT? BE MY GUIDE?

34

TURN TO PAGE 61.

'I, uh . . . I guess I'll join up, then.'

'Fine,' the thief says. 'Emil, you go back to your group and keep covering for us. You — come with me.'

You follow the thief into another room. The other men are in there, carrying boxes filled with gold through a door and up a narrow ramp to the outside.

'Take that one and go after them,' the thief tells you. You grab the box and fall in line . . .

. . . but when you emerge you're suddenly grabbed and forced down to the ground! Your hands are twisted around and handcuffed.

The Egyptian cop hauls you to your feet. 'Tomb robbers, eh?' You look around and see the other thieves nearby, also cuffed. 'You'll do thirty years for this!'

As you're taken away in the police car, you can't help but think: Your parents are going to be so disappointed with your behaviour on this expedition.

THE END

You'd love to get out of here. Those thieves scare you to pieces. But that sarcophagus just looks *incredibly* cool. You tiptoe towards it.

The carving on the lid is so realistic. It's like the queen's carved eyes are looking right into yours . . . and you feel almost hypnotised. That's when you realise that you actually can't move. Your feet won't work . . . ! And so you have no choice but to stand there and watch . . .

. . . while the sarcophagus lid starts to open. You can't even scream when the mummy inside leans forward and looks at you . . .

GO ON TO THE NEXT PAGE.

GO ON TO THE NEXT PAGE.

TWISTED JOURNEYS®

What have you got yourself into?

WILL YOU . . .

. . . graciously accept this 'gift'?
TURN TO PAGE 76.

. . . politely thank the nice mummy but tell her no?
TURN TO PAGE 57.

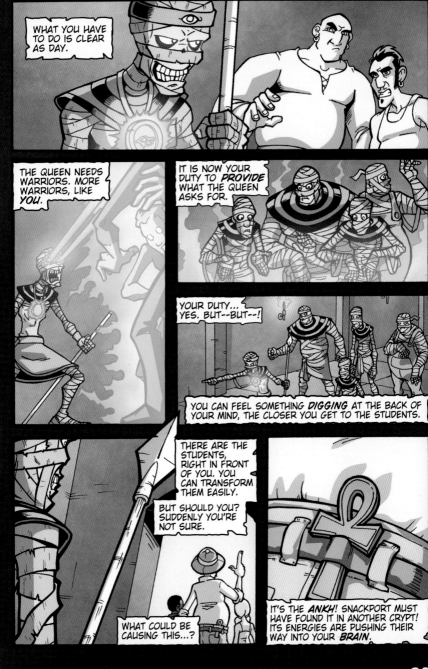

WHAT YOU HAVE TO DO IS CLEAR AS DAY.

THE QUEEN NEEDS WARRIORS. MORE WARRIORS, LIKE *YOU*.

IT IS NOW YOUR DUTY TO *PROVIDE* WHAT THE QUEEN ASKS FOR.

YOUR DUTY... YES. BUT--BUT--!

YOU CAN FEEL SOMETHING *DIGGING* AT THE BACK OF YOUR MIND, THE CLOSER YOU GET TO THE STUDENTS.

THERE ARE THE STUDENTS, RIGHT IN FRONT OF YOU. YOU CAN TRANSFORM THEM EASILY.

BUT SHOULD YOU? SUDDENLY YOU'RE NOT SURE.

WHAT COULD BE CAUSING THIS...?

IT'S THE *ANKH*! SNACKPORT MUST HAVE FOUND IT IN ANOTHER CRYPT! ITS ENERGIES ARE PUSHING THEIR WAY INTO YOUR *BRAIN*.

GO ON TO THE NEXT PAGE.

You're filled with the need to obey the queen . . . but the ankh makes you remember that these are your fellow students. It's so hard to decide what to do!

WILL YOU . . .

. . . transform the students so they can join you and the thieves?
TURN TO PAGE 58.

. . . rush to tell the students what's happening so you can defend them?
TURN TO PAGE 98.

. . . turn around and attack the thieves?
TURN TO PAGE 74.

'Wake up now,' you whisper in the mummy's dried-up ear. 'Please . . . ?'

'Your efforts are useless,' says a rough, growling voice. You whirl around to see the first mummy enter the room.

'Wrong as always,' says the second mummy, climbing out of his sarcophagus.

'*Guardian*,' snarls the first mummy. 'How can this be? You were never this powerful before!'

'I've grown stronger,' the Guardian says. 'Let me show you.'

Blinding beams of light spring out of the Guardian's eyes and wash over the first mummy. He screams as his bandages burst into flames – and then he's gone. Vanished in a cloud of fine ash.

The Guardian turns to look at you . . .

. . . and abruptly you and the rest of the students are standing outside the pyramid.

You hear the Guardian's voice: *Do not come back inside. You are forbidden.*

'Well.' Professor Snackport clears his throat. 'I suppose this expedition will be marked . . . Incomplete.'

THE END

You push through the curtain and take a few steps forward. You're trying to look as tough as you can. 'Who are you guys? What're you doing here?'

Judging by the thieves' reactions, your attempt at being tough has failed miserably.

'Grab that kid!' one of them shouts. You try to turn and run, but you get tangled up in the curtain. For a second you can't even tell which way is up . . .

. . . and then they've got you! You try to shout out — but one of them stuffs a rag in your mouth. It tastes like sawdust.

'This solves our problem, eh, boys?'

You'd really like to know what they meant by that.

Looks as if you've got no choice.
You're going to have to push a switch.

WILL YOU CHOOSE . . .

. . . the sarcophagus?
TURN TO PAGE 87.

. . . the cat's head?
TURN TO PAGE 32.

. . . the mummy glyph?
TURN TO PAGE 48.

You realise you
can't actually talk
anymore . . . but that's not
really necessary. You wind
around the priestess's ankles
and start to purr.

Purring feels surpris-
ingly good, too.

She picks you up, cradles
you in her arms and starts stroking your head
between the ears. This cat stuff is all right! 'There's a
good kitty,' the priestess says soothingly.

She waves her hand. 'Let me show you your new
home.' Part of the wall opens up, revealing a secret passageway. She strides down it, keeping you in her arms.

As she goes you can feel her flesh expanding — her skin
growing softer and smoother. A minute later she walks
out into a large, dark room. When she waves her hand
again, torches light up around the walls.

GO ON TO THE NEXT PAGE.

'This way!' the professor bellows.

Through twists and turns you follow Professor Snackport, but you can still hear the mummy behind you. Rotten cloth dragging on stone . . . it's getting closer!

Then suddenly you burst out of the pyramid into the night air. You're outside and nothing's following you out! You think everything's going to be okay . . .

. . . until you see the bizarre look in Professor Snackport's eyes.

'Professor?' you ask. 'Are you all right?'

'This is all *your* fault!' he screams, and you realise: Professor Snackport has just gone totally crazy.

'See what lack of preparation does? *See?* What sort of student are you? You've *failed* this class! Do you hear me? *I'm calling your parents!*'

Nothing you can do or say makes any difference. The professor has gone off the deep end and one phone call later, you'll be on another plane back home.

But at least you're alive . . .

THE END

You reach a hand out. Mummy? Cat? Coffin? Well, you are in Egypt. In a *pyramid*. Shouldn't you be doing *something* with mummies?

You press the mummy symbol and hear a sharp click.

Suddenly you're falling! The floor has given way!

You're zooming down a chute of some kind, leaving the pedestal and the thieves far behind you. The chute dumps you out in a dimly lit room . . .

. . . and there's a mummy sitting on a golden throne right in the middle of it!

You get to your feet. It's okay – it's just a mummy, right? Mummies are dead. They can't hurt you.

You start to look around for a way out. There aren't any doors. Maybe something around the mummy's throne?

But as you get closer to the throne . . . the mummy's head turns! You're not imagining it – it's really moving. The mummy raises one hand towards you . . .

GO ON TO THE NEXT PAGE.

TWISTED JOURNEYS®

How is this thing moving? Mummies are supposed to be dead! Maybe . . . maybe it's a hoax, but you're not sure.

WILL YOU . . .

. . . frantically try to climb back up the chute you fell down?
TURN TO PAGE 70.

. . . confront the mummy and demand an explanation?
TURN TO PAGE 34.

The thieves are barely worth your effort. They flee the pyramid, screaming as they go.

But they're not the ones you really want to focus on. They're not the ones determined to poke and prod and take this pyramid apart. You want the students you came here with and the tall man . . . the professor! It is they who have offended you and your mistress most deeply. They think they can understand the ancient mysteries? How *dare* they?

You discover that you *know* this pyramid now. Every hallway, every chamber. It takes you only minutes to catch up with the group.

They don't see you at first. You smile. This ought to be fun.

You can feel the professor's influence
chipping away at the queen's hold on you!

WILL YOU . . .

. . . help the professor and try to resist the
queen's power?
TURN TO PAGE 66.

. . . dedicate yourself to your new mission
and fight the professor?
TURN TO PAGE 109.

You whip the amulet off the mummy and slide it over the professor's head – and his eyes start glowing.

'Professor? Are you all right?'

His eyes glow more brightly. The professor gestures – and part of the wall opens up. There's a long, dark tunnel behind it. 'Go!' he says. 'Take the other children and go! I must stay here. *I* am the Guardian now. Go! He's almost here!'

You gather the other students and head for the tunnel just as the first mummy enters the room. It growls and charges towards the professor.

You and the other children run as fast as you can . . .

. . . and then you're outside! The wall where you came out is smooth – like there was never a door there at all.

You know this expedition is finished.

You just don't know what you're going to tell people about Professor Snackport . .

.

THE END

You hurry to catch up with the rest of the group. Professor Snackport leads you into a big, square room with a huge golden coffin in the middle of the floor. The lid is carved to look like a man in ancient Egyptian clothing with his arms crossed over his chest.

'Who can tell me what this is?' the professor asks.

You timidly raise your hand. 'A sarcophagus?'

'Very good!' He gives you a toothy smile. 'It's a sarcophagus — a burial container, in which lies an ancient Egyptian mummy.'

A low murmur runs through the group. A *mummy?* The kid on your right says, 'Coool!'

Professor Snackport continues talking about the sarcophagus. For a minute you listen closely. But then . . .

. . . then you *see* something.

Or at least you *think* you do.

You rub your eyes. Maybe you imagined it?

GO ON TO THE NEXT PAGE.

TWISTED JOURNEYS®

You've never seen anything like that before!

WILL YOU . . .

. . . immediately tell Professor Snackport
what you saw?

TURN TO PAGE 26.

. . . stay behind in the room and get
a better look at the sarcophagus?

TURN TO PAGE 82.

'I really, really appreciate the offer,' you begin. 'But I don't think it would be right for me to accept a *gift* . . . '

She frowns.

'I gave you the choice because I am *polite,*' she says as she walks around you. 'No one has *ever* rejected a gift from the High Priestess of Bast.' The green glow from her sceptre gets a lot brighter. 'I'm afraid I'm going to have to see to it that this is both the first and the *last* time that happens.'

In an instant you feel all thoughts leave your mind. You only want one thing now: to do the mummy's bidding. Nothing else matters. Nothing in the world.

'Follow me, my servant,' the priestess says. 'We have much to do.'

'Yes, mistress,' you say dully. 'I live to serve you. Now and forever.'

You shuffle along behind her, following the mummy into darkness.

THE END

58

The creature that used to be Professor Snackport steps forward. Even as a mummy warrior, he looks a little too gawky to be truly frightening.

'What are your orders?' he asks you. For a second, you forget you're a mummy — it's weird to give commands to a professor!

But you don't let it affect your mission. 'Follow me.'

You lead your mummy troops up and out of Pyramid X. The guide is still waiting for you outside. 'Oh my word!' she begins. You mummify her in a heartbeat. She falls in line with the rest of your troops.

The sand crunches under your feet as you head away from the pyramid. In the distance — the far distance — you can see the lights of a city. The queen's voice whispers in your mind: *Go, my warrior! Bring me new soldiers for my army!*

GO ON TO THE NEXT PAGE.

It takes hours to walk all the way to the city. When you finally get there the sun's about to come up . . . but that doesn't stop you.

You and your warrior troops march through the city like a tidal wave, wrecking or transforming everything in your path. Civilians, police even the army — no one can stand up to your mystical power.

Yes! you hear the queen whisper in your mind. *Take them all — take everything! All of it will be mine! Mine!*

And so it goes — city after city. Days stretch into weeks. Weeks become months. And the queen's army continues to grow. Soon enough she will become ruler of the Earth.

Of course, it'll be an Earth populated entirely by mummies . . . but you don't care! You think it sounds like a fantastic plan.

Especially since, except for the queen, *you're* in charge.

THE END

This is like no mummy you've ever seen in the cinema! He seems pretty sincere. But then again, he's been dead for a *really* long time.

WILL YOU . . .

. . . try to think of some way to say 'no' and still be polite?

TURN TO PAGE 93.

. . . agree to show Prince Amenhotep around the modern world?

TURN TO PAGE 85.

THERE'S NO TIME TO DEBATE THIS! EVERYONE, COME WITH ME!

THE PROFESSOR LEADS THE GROUP INTO A SMALL, CRAMPED TUNNEL. IT'S ALL YOU CAN DO JUST TO KEEP UP WITH THE KID IN FRONT OF YOU...

...AND YOU BREATHE A SIGH OF RELIEF AS YOU FINALLY SEE THE TUNNEL ENDING UP AHEAD.

THE WHOLE TIME YOU'VE IMAGINED YOU COULD FEEL THE MUMMY'S BREATH ON THE BACK OF YOUR NECK.

PROFESSOR? WHAT IS THIS PLACE?

IT'S THE MUMMY'S *ARMY*! BURIED HERE WITH HIM-- MAYBE EVEN BURIED *ALIVE*!?

OF COURSE, ONCE YOU SEE WHERE YOU ARE, YOU'RE NOT SURE YOU WOULDN'T RATHER BE FACING THE MUMMY!

You point at the two doorways at the back of the room. 'Can we get out that way, Professor? Which door should we take?'

Professor Snackport stares at the symbols above the doors. One is very similar to the design on the mummy's amulet. The other looks like a fist holding a glowing rod. The professor bites one of his knuckles and squints his eyes.

'I don't know . . . I don't know which one to take.'

Just then somebody screams! You whirl around to see the mummy climb out of the tunnel. Everybody scrambles away from him and clusters around you and the professor. Ming grabs your hand and holds on tight.

'Awaken,' the mummy grates out. 'Awaken, my soldiers! Awaken and serve me once more!'

For a moment you don't realise what's happening. There's sound all around you — grinding, scraping. Then you see it. The sarcophagus doors are opening.

All of them.

GO ON TO THE NEXT PAGE.

There's no choice but to take one of the two doorways.

WILL YOU . . .

. . . take the one with the fist holding
the glowing rod?
TURN TO PAGE 106.

. . . take the one with the mummy's amulet above it?
TURN TO PAGE 14.

You leave the mummy and the sarcophagus behind and sprint down the hallway and back out the entrance. The guide is still there and is quite surprised to see you.

'Are you all right?' she asks. 'Want to ask a question?'

'No!' you shout. 'Just get me out of here! I want to go home!'

•••••

It's the next day, and you're waiting to get on a plane. Professor Snackport shows up to see you off.

You roll your eyes. Of course he didn't believe you about the mummy. No one did. But you don't care! All you want is to get back home and stay there.

'This really is too bad,' the professor says. 'You could have had a great adventure on this expedition.'

'I'll stick to books, thanks,' you answer. You've had more than enough adventure for one lifetime.

THE END

'What am I *doing?*' you ask in a weak voice. The ankh gets closer and closer to you and you find yourself pulling strength from it.

'Resist!' says Professor Snackport. 'Resist the ancient power!'

You're trying with everything you've got . . . and then you feel something in your mind snap. The spear clangs to the floor, then *vanishes* and you slump to the ground.

'Somebody call an ambulance!' you hear Snackport shout . . .

. . . . .

So the last bit of your visit is spent in hospital. You're okay – just a bit dried out. 'Your parents don't need to know about this . . . ahem . . . *mummy* business if you don't want them to,' the professor tells you.

Yes. You think that might be for the best.

THE END

YOU'VE GOT TO GET BACK AND TELL THE PROFESSOR! THESE GUYS ARE *THIEVES* --THEY COULD BE *DANGEROUS*!

WELL, AREN'T YOU THE NOSY ONE.

HEY-- HEY!

SCREAM IF YOU WANT.

SOUND DOES NOT TRAVEL THROUGH THICK STONE WALLS.

THE THIEF THROWS YOU OVER HIS SHOULDER AND *CARRIES* YOU. YOU CAN'T TELL HOW FAR.

YOU CAN HEAR THE FOUR OTHER THIEVES FOLLOWING ALONG BEHIND HIM, MURMURING AMONG THEMSELVES.

AND AFTER WHAT SEEMS LIKE SEVERAL MINUTES, HE SETS YOU DOWN ON THE FLOOR. YOU HEAR HIM AND THE OTHER MEN WALK AWAY.

THAT'S WHEN YOU NOTICE THE TINY LITTLE *TEAR* IN THE SACK . . .

The thieves are gone — and you think maybe you could make that rip bigger.

WILL YOU . . .

. . . ignore what the thief said and scream your head off?

TURN TO PAGE 16.

. . . tear your way out of the sack?

TURN TO PAGE 8.

Something's happening to you. Something *strange*. These bandages feel good – snug. Just the way they're supposed to feel.

And these trembling students in front of you have *no business* here!

'Graaaahhgh!' The roar surprises you as it comes out of your mouth. But then . . . you decide you *like* the way it sounds.

'Run!' Professor Snackport shouts. 'Run, get out, get out! It's going to kill us all!'

You chase the students and the professor down the main hallway. Seeing them so scared makes you happy . . . because this is *your* home now. As they run outside you touch a switch on the wall – a switch you *knew* would be there. A huge stone slab slides down across the doorway, sealing it permanently.

You turn and shamble back into the pyramid. Everything is dark now. Dark and quiet.

Just the way you like it.

THE END

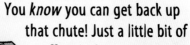

You *know* you can get back up that chute! Just a little bit of effort and you can wriggle right back up to the room with the pedestal . . .

Wow, these walls are really slippery . . .

And then a hand clamps down on your shoulder.

'Where did you think you were going?' the mummy snarls. 'You wake me up and then try to run away?'

'I didn't mean to wake anybody up!' you shout. But it's not listening and it grabs you by the throat.

'You'll be coming with me,' the mummy says – and to your horror, you feel your body shrinking, narrowing, turning into . . .

. . . a snake.

You twine around the neck and shoulders of your new master. 'Come now, my pet,' the mummy says. 'Let us go and explore this new world. The world that we shall conquer . . . together.'

THE END

PROFESSOR WHAT DO YOU THINK ABOUT THIS AMULET UP HERE?

WHAT DOES IT MEAN?

AMULET?

OH! OH, MY YES! THAT *IS* AN AMULET, ISN'T IT?

EARLY FOURTH DYNASTY, I'D SAY...

OR POSSIBLY MIDDLE KINGDOM... I'LL NEED TO

-OOAAAH!

DO NOT TOUCH ME.

AAAAAAHH!

GO ON TO THE NEXT PAGE.

Professor Snackport quickly-jerks his hand out of the mummy's grasp and jumps backwards . . .

. . . then turns and grabs *you*. 'We have to go!' the professor shouts. You look around – and see the mummy starting to climb out of the sarcophagus. He looks angry. *Really* angry. 'We have to go right this very instant!'

Then you can't tell what else the mummy's doing, because the professor is dragging you along with him. He runs into the passage the rest of the students went down . . .

. . . but then turns down another side passage. This place looks unstable – thick beams of wood are holding up the ceiling. As you pass one you bump into it and it falls to the floor with a loud crash.

You risk a look behind you – and there's the mummy! He's chasing you and he's catching up *fast*.

You're not sure you can outrun this thing!

WILL YOU . . .

. . . keep running and hope you can escape it?

TURN TO PAGE 47.

. . . stop and face it,
determined to fight?

TURN TO PAGE 25.

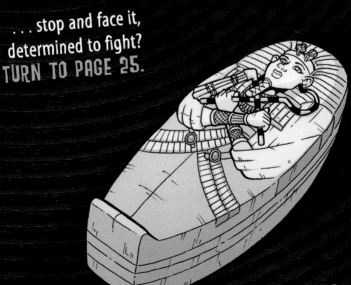

GO ON TO THE NEXT PAGE.

It's a crypt chamber that you're driving the thief mummies towards. Get them in there, seal them in. Then you can worry about exactly what's going to happen to you.

'Leader, please!' one of them cries out. 'Why are you doing this? We are loyal to you!'

You don't answer as you finish forcing all of them into the crypt chamber. Now . . . to hit the switch next to the door and seal them in permanently. . .

Then two things happen at once. You hit the switch . . . but one of the mummies grabs hold of you and pulls you into the chamber as the door slides down! You can't get out the door fast enough . . .

. . . and it closes. You're sealed in with them!

The thief mummies turn on you. They don't look happy at all.

But hey, at least the other kids are safe! And they'll come looking for you eventually. Right?

Right?

THE END

You're not sure what you're letting yourself in for . . . but you don't want to make the priestess angry!

'I would, uh, gladly accept any gift you have to offer,' you mumble. She looks pleased.

'Very good,' she says. The glow from her sceptre gets brighter. 'I shall transform you into the most perfect of all shapes — a cat!'

Your eyes get huge when you hear her words — and then you can feel your pupils grow narrow and slitted. The rest of you changes, too. Your body shrinks, fur sprouts all over you . . .

. . . and you can feel your long, graceful tail waving back and forth.

It actually feels *nice*.

'Now,' the priestess says. 'Soon I shall restore my own body. Then I want you to agree to work for me and be my faithful servant. Will you do what I ask of you?'

GO ON TO THE NEXT PAGE.

You've never felt stranger in your life . . . but you get the feeling that being a cat might not be all that bad! The question is,

WILL YOU . . .

. . . agree to work for the priestess?
TURN TO PAGE 45.

. . . run away as fast as you can?
TURN TO PAGE 81.

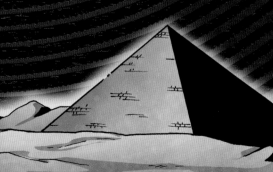

GO ON TO THE NEXT PAGE.

In seconds you overtake the thieves.

You force them at spear-point into the room where they've hidden all of the loot they took from the pyramid. One by one, they empty the boxes and sacks.

'*Now,*' you growl. It makes them whimper some more. '*Get out of my home!*'

They don't need to be told a second time. Screaming for their lives, they run out of the pyramid into the desert night as fast as their legs can carry them. You watch them go, satisfied.

GO ON TO THE NEXT PAGE.

Suddenly, you feel another change! The spear in your hand vanishes . . . Your clothes go back to normal . . . Your flesh fills in again and your skin becomes soft.

You're back! Just like you were when you walked into this place. What just *happened?*

You hear the voice from the statue. It whispers in your head one last time . . .

Thank you. Then it's gone. You're alone.

As you're walking back towards the student group, you can't help but say out loud: 'Nobody's *ever* going to believe this.'

THE END

81

You follow along with the rest of the students as they file out of the room . . . but at the last second you hang back and step to one side of the doorway.

Nobody notices you're not with the group anymore. You listen and hear the sounds of their footsteps and voices fade as they move away.

Now it's just you and that sarcophagus. . .

You creep closer. The gold and blue decorations on the lid glow and glimmer in the dim light. Even though you saw the lid move, you're still not completely sure.

'H-hello?' you whisper. 'Is anybody in there?'

Your voice echoes softly around the room.

The only sound is your own breathing . . .

. . . but then stone begins to grind on stone!

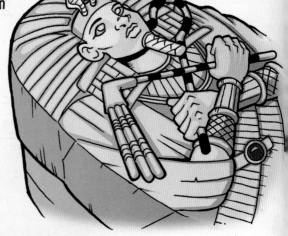

GO ON TO THE NEXT PAGE.

Your blood freezes with terror.

WILL YOU . . .

. . . scream as loud as you can?
TURN TO PAGE 30.

. . . run as fast as your feet will take you?
TURN TO PAGE 65.

. . . leap to your feet and slam the
sarcophagus lid shut?
TURN TO PAGE 102.

The two of you become a worldwide sensation in no time.

Professor Snackport is completely in awe of Prince Amenhotep. But that's nothing compared with how much the reporters love him! Within three days the prince's picture is on the front page of every newspaper on the planet . . .

. . . and you're right there with him. You're 'the kid who found the mummy.' Your whole life changes.

The two of you show up all over the place. You're on the evening news. You're on talk shows. You're on the front of cereal boxes. Now they're even talking about making a TV show about you.

Life is good. Even if one of you has been dead for three or four thousand years.

THE END

Looking at the statue for a few seconds makes you completely forget about the thieves behind you. You hear them turn and run out of the room.

Then a voice comes out of the statue — dry and crackling like autumn leaves.

'I have changed my mind about you,' it says. 'I was going to mummify you. But instead . . . I think I shall make you an even more permanent companion.'

The bandages drop away. You can feel your flesh and bones start to *change* again. What's happening to you?

But then you realise what's happening: *You're turning into a statue too!*

Seconds later it's over. Now *two* statues stand alone in the crypt . . . the queen and another, standing in her shadow.

The queen has some company now. The kind that never leaves.

Ever.

THE END

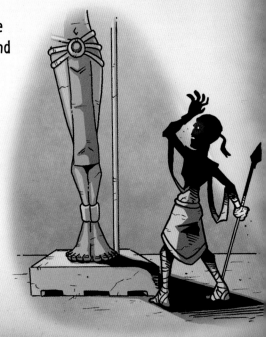

A CHOICE AT RANDOM--ONE OUT OF THREE CHANCES. THIS ONE'S AS GOOD AS ANY OF THE OTHERS, RIGHT?

LOOK AT *THAT!* EXCELLENT!

GOOD JOB, KID.

NOW YOU GET TO COME WITH US--AND PUSH ANY *OTHER* SWITCHES WE FIND.

GREAT. THIS IS *HARDLY* WHAT YOU WANTED OUT OF A SCHOOL TRIP.

HEY--THAT AMULET IS *COOL.* AND YOU'RE CLOSE ENOUGH...

...TO JUST REACH RIGHT OUT AND *TAKE* IT. YOU BET NOBODY WOULD EVEN NOTICE, THEY'RE SO EXCITED ABOUT THESE *STAIRS.*

TURN TO PAGE 101.

You slam the door shut, then brace it closed with a wooden plank. Immediately the thieves start whamming against the door. 'Open this door! Let us out of here or we'll skin you alive!'

But you've done it! They're trapped, going nowhere.

• • • • •

Forty-five minutes later: You, the professor and the other students stand outside Pyramid X and watch as the thieves are loaded into a police wagon.

'Well done!' says Professor Snackport. He claps a hand onto your shoulder. 'Well done indeed! You'll get a reward for this!'

Then the professor dusts his hands off and turns back to the pyramid. 'But enough of that. We've still got plenty of work to do. And *no straying from the group* this time, yes?'

You follow the professor back inside with your shoulders slumped.

At least your adventure was fun while it lasted!

THE END

Aaaahh! You're a *mouse?* You *hate* mice!

But you know that mice can run really fast – and that's exactly what you do. Your tiny little hairless feet take you whizzing down the corridor away from that awful mummy . . .

. . . but the stairs are too high! You can't climb up!

That's when you hear the sound from behind you . . . the low rumbling growl . . .

. . . of *cats.*

You look back the way you came and see the mummy standing in the doorway. Twining around her feet are five big, lean, terrifying cats!

'Go, my pets,' the mummy says quietly. 'Show the intruder what happens to those who trouble us.'

You're literally trapped like a rat . . . and as you watch the cats pad down the hallway towards you, you realise that this is. . .

. . . THE END

'This way! Come on, let's *go!*' You push and pull the other students after you. Professor Snackport is already through the door with the hand-and-rod symbol above it. You have to catch up with him!

You and the other children run like crazy. The corridor you find yourself in twists and turns like a wet piece of spaghetti . . .

. . . and soon you reach the end of the hallway and spill out into a chamber larger than any you've seen before.

There's another sarcoph-agus in the middle of the floor. This one has the hand-and-rod symbol carved all the way around it. Professor Snackport is just standing there, staring at it. You speak to him.

'Professor? *Professor?* Shouldn't we be getting out of here? Like, *right away?*' He looks over at you. It's clear his mind is somewhere else.

You're barely in control of your own actions — the pull of the amulet is so strong! You know this mummy is somehow incredibly important.

WILL YOU . . .

. . . take the amulet and put it on yourself?
TURN TO PAGE 31.

. . . take the amulet and put it around the professor's neck?
TURN TO PAGE 53.

. . . shake the mummy and try to wake it up?
TURN TO PAGE 41.

. . . break the amulet's hold on your mind and slam the lid shut?
TURN TO PAGE 89.

Forget the professor and his stupid ankh! You've got a job to do! You snarl and start forwards.

But then the professor shouts: 'Push! Everyone, push toward the sarcophagus!'

You're surrounded — hands grab your arms and legs — and you're shoved straight towards the open coffin! You struggle, fling away one student, then another . . .

. . . but there are too many of them. They slam you into the sarcophagus and hold you there. *'You can't do this!'* you snarl at them. *'My queen is far, far more powerful than you will ever be!'*

The professor looms over you. 'Not terribly convincing just now.'

Then he slams the lid shut, sealing you in. You try to get out, but you can't — it won't open at all.

You've failed your queen . . . and you can feel sleep stealing over you. The kind of sleep that lasts a long, long time. . .

THE END

You've had enough of these thieves — and as you stagger towards them, you feel an odd surge of strength rush through you. You could really hurt these guys. Maybe you *will*.

Two of them turn and run away in the first few seconds. The other two stay, determined to stand their ground.

· · · · ·

Hours later, Professor Snackport leads the student group into the room. 'Fascinating, just fascinating!' he's saying. 'I don't remember this on the map at all! I – oh, good heavens!'

You know what he's seeing: three mummies, lying there on the floor around the statue of the queen. You've turned the two thieves into mummies . . . and now the three of you will sleep the eternal sleep of the pharaohs. This fate awaits *any* who would rob the pyramid.

You close your eyes, feeling peaceful and let the sleep overtake you.

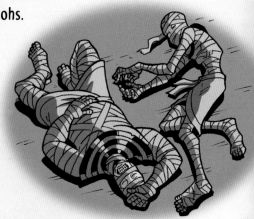

THE END

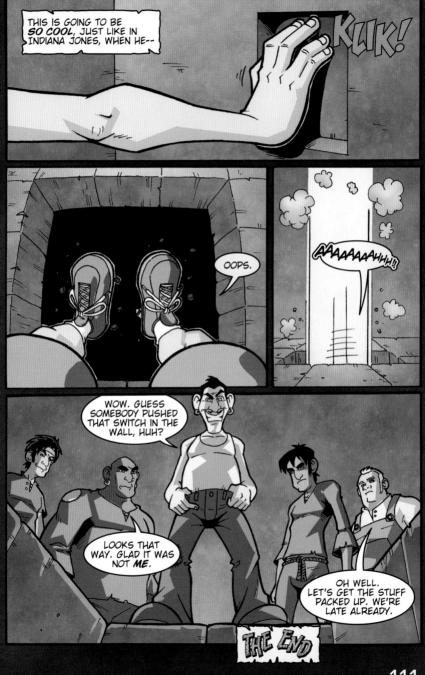

READY FOR MORE ADVENTURES?

WHICH TWISTED JOURNEYS®

WILL YOU TRY NEXT?

#1 CAPTURED BY PIRATES
Danger on the high seas! A band of scurvy pirates has boarded your ship. Can you keep them from turning you into shark bait?

#2 ESCAPE FROM PYRAMID X
You're on an archaeological mission to an ancient pyramid, complete with ancient mummies. Unfortunately for you, not everything that's ancient is also dead...

#3 TERROR IN GHOST MANSION
Halloween's not supposed to be this scary. You and your friends are trapped in a creepy old house with a family of ghosts. And they definitely aren't wearing costumes...

#4 THE TREASURE OF MOUNT FATE
Plenty of people have braved the monsters and magic of Mount Fate in search of its legendary treasure. But no one has ever lived to tell about their quest. Will you be the first?

This book was first published in the United States of America in 2007.
Text copyright © 2007 by Lerner Publishing Group, Inc.